What Would Jesus Want You to Eat?

I love the phrase, "What Would Jesus Do?"

It's a great question to live by.

The idea for the now-infamous bracelet with this question on it was God-inspired.

I buy "WWJD" bracelets in packages of 50 to share with friends and family.

These bracelets inspire and motivate believers and non-believers alike.

"What would Jesus do?" is a great question that can lead to some interesting discussion.

It helps you think about Jesus Christ. Who He is. What He said. What He stood for. And most important; what He would want you to do in any situation.

Because Jesus is God, asking this question helps lead you to the right thoughts that God would want for you.

Wearing a 'WWJD' bracelet and reminding yourself of this question leads you to a life that is <u>focused</u> on Jesus Christ and what He wants for you.

This will affect your thoughts and actions.

For me, when I look at the bracelet on my own wrist, I ask myself:

What would Jesus say about the food I eat?

More generally, what would Jesus say if He walked into a modern grocery store and saw the ingredients in the food that you and I are piling into our carts?

Would He approve of these overly processed, pre-packaged foods?

And what would He think about fast-food restaurants?

And all the sugar and other chemical ingredients we put into our bodies?

That's a question I'll attempt to answer. I don't think that Jesus would approve of a lot of the foods that most of us eat. However, I think He would approve of this diet. Because this diet is focused on what Jesus would want you to eat.

Instead of 'WWJD' – the acronym for The Jesus Diet is...

" W W J W Y T E "

When it comes to your diet, think "What Would Jesus Want You To Eat?

Would He want you to eat junk food?

Would He want you to eat the over-processed foods that are sold in grocery stores?

Would he approve of all the chemical ingredients that are

added to modern-day pre-packaged foods?

I think you know the answer.

So what is The Jesus Diet? And why is it more important today than ever before?

Well, to begin to answer this question, read this...

"Imagine a world where politicians, in league with corporations, pursue their own interests with no genuine concern for the lives or livelihoods of the people they claim to serve. Imagine a world where, instead of trusting and empowering individuals to look after themselves and their families, politicians and corporations foster extreme dependency by peddling ad-hoc treatments instead of solutions to the underlying problems; where the public are stuffed with Frankenstein foods and dosed with pills, while the nutritious life-preserving foods that sustained their ancestors for millennia are slandered and treated as the opposite. Now imagine a world where this twisted regime does all these things and more in open furtherance of a plan to destroy the nations and usher in a new global form of government, a form of tyranny that will be unlike any seen before.

Well, you don't have to imagine any of this, because this is what's actually taking place here, now, more or less wherever you live. This is "soy globalism" and it is the opposite of everything The Jesus Diet stands for."

The above statement was published by a group of people who call themselves 'Raw Egg Nationalists'... I replaced their name with "Jesus Diet" for impact.

Those 177 words are so powerful. And they ring true in my heart.

Just like the acronym "WWJD" – I believe these words are God-inspired! I read them and instantly saw the truth. See if you don't agree. Please read everything in the box a few times. Study those words. Keep coming back to them again. And see if you don't agree with me when I say that it's a no-brainer that...

Jesus wants you to eat the very best food.

Good health and good living starts with your diet. According to many experts, the modern foods we eat are making us fat, sick, and even depressed.

Jesus does <u>not</u> want you to eat food that makes you fat, depressed, and sick.

Think about it: It's <u>the</u> <u>enemy</u> – the great deceiver – who wants you to stay sick.

This is extremely important, because...

The devil is <u>active</u> in the food and drug industry. This is <u>not</u> necessarily an evil industry, but it does benefit from a market of fat, unhappy, depressed, isolated, and sick people.

Think about it this way: The more everyone is healthy, happy, and joined together, the less money they can make. The unhappier their shareholders are. That's the truth.

They don't want to kill you, because the money train will stop. But they definitely don't want you to be healthy, happy and full of life... things that Jesus wants for you!

To these businesses, you are a cash cow that they want to milk. They benefit greatly from a population of people who are overweight, sick, unhappy, and weak.

This makes it easier for them to control us.

It's how they divide us.

It's a way to make money off us.

It's how they manipulate us.

And it's how they stay in power.

Does all that sound like a vast right-wing conspiracy? You know in your heart that it's not. Think about all of this and then ask yourself...

"What would Jesus want for me?"

God has a unique plan for you. And that plan does not include being fat, depressed, miserable, isolated, and sick.

The foods we eat play a key role in our health and well-being. Whoever said "you are what you eat" was only half-right. The more accurate statement goes like this:

"You are What You Eat is Doing to You!"

Today's overprocessed food is loaded with chemical ingredients that most medical authorities have never even heard of. Everything has cornstarch in it (which is a deadly form of sugar). They add way too much salt and sugar to these products.

All of this is making us terribly unhealthy.

Many of these modern foods are making us fat, unhappy, depressed, and sick.

And the 10 companies behind nearly 100% of the pre-packaged food we buy are to blame. Yes, according to Business Insider, just 10 corporations – General Mills, Kellogg's, Associated British Foods, Mondolez, Mars, Danone, Unilever, Coca-Cola, Nestle, and Pepsico – control almost every large food and beverage brand in the entire world.

That's how they make money. It's how they gain more power.

Consider this: The more people on this planet who are overweight, sick, and isolated from each other, the more they will have total power over us.

That's not a conspiracy, it's the truth.

I don't blame you for being skeptical. But I am not some wild-eyed conspiracy thinker... I am a person with a general distrust of authority. In fact, I believe you can usually do the opposite of what the people in power tell you to do, and you'll be okay.

More about that later... For right now, let me answer this question...

What is The Jesus Diet and why should you make it a vital part of your life?

The Jesus Diet is a form of Intermittent Fasting.

Have you heard about Intermittent Fasting? If so, you know that this is a diet that generally lets you eat what you want and still lose weight.

This is a diet focused on when you eat and not what you eat.

I'll give you all the details in this. Once you understand the basics, I think you'll be impressed, to put it mildly.

As you'll see, this diet can change your life. And it can change the lives of the people you love. It can also change the lives of billions of other people. And I am going to show you how you can make money by helping me share The Jesus Diet with as many people as possible. Much more on that later. For now, know this:

The benefit of eating what you love and losing weight is what initially attracts people to this diet. But for Christians, it's different. The Apostle Paul said in 1st Corinthians 10:23 (Jesus Diet Paraphrase), *"Everything is permissible to eat, but not everything is beneficial."* Yes, you "can" eat whatever you want. But I believe there are so many processed foods that Jesus would not want us to eat.

Because of this, The Jesus Diet places a much higher emphasis on healthy eating.

Your diet is the foundation of your health and wellness. Modern diets are leading to disease and death. They're making people fat, sick, and even depressed. Once you realize this great truth, then you will realize the next one, which is the fact that...

Jesus does not want you
to make yourself sick.

This diet is also focused on the spiritual aspects of fasting.

Fasting has been around for thousands of years. Jesus himself fasted. And nutrition experts say that this regular type of daily fasting can help you experience many of the same benefits of long-term fasting.

What would Jesus really want for you? If you're like me, you ask yourself that question. And I believe the answer is slightly different for each of us. A Christian mystic once said, "God leads every soul by a separate path." I believe that is true. However, for now let's focus on something most of us can easily agree on.

Jesus came to heal. He wants people to be healthy and experience overall well-being, including spiritual wellness.

This diet is for Christians or anyone else who wants to learn more about Jesus and what he might want us to eat.

There's an emphasis on the spiritual elements of fasting, it's a way to draw closer to Jesus and learn more about Him. And that's why we included a short prayer for people who have not invited Jesus to come into their lives.

In the Gospel of John, Jesus said this:

> "The thief comes only to steal and kill and destroy; I came so that they would have life and have it abundantly."

What could that mean? Jesus made two analogies about His ministry using a topic that was very familiar to His listeners: Shepherding. The first relied on the idea that sheep instinctively listened only to the voice of their own shepherd, and no other. This, Jesus implies, is why His religious critics reject Him: They are part of another flock.

In the second idea, Jesus claims to be "the door." He was talking about the single narrow opening in sheep pens of His day. This was the way the sheep were able to come and go from their pen. Jesus's detractors, then, are like thieves and robbers who try to take the sheep without using that door.

The purpose of a thief, so far as a flock of sheep is concerned, is only to wreak havoc; to cause mayhem to get what he wants. In the same way, ungodly people who claim to be spiritual cause suffering in others for the sake of their pride and greed.

In contrast, Jesus seeks to not just preserve life, but to provide it.

In the analogy of the sheep, Jesus claimed that as THE one and only door, He was the means by which a person could be saved. The Greek term for that word, suggests rescue, protection, and healing.

Here, Jesus deepens that claim by saying that His purpose is not only tied to life, but to an abundant life.

Up to $234 in Free Gifts at JesusDietChallenge.com

Hear me out. The "abundant life" is not some cheap prosperity gospel. No, it means something more than material wealth and prosperity. It begins with salvation from an eternity of suffering the penalty of sin and separation from God.

An abundant life is, first and foremost, eternal life. An abundant life means gaining a heavenly perspective, leading to a growing trust and knowledge of God. It means blossoming into a life full of the fruit of the spirit. False teachers and false religions offer version of life that are shallow, that offer temporary relief. Only Jesus brings truly everlasting life and spiritual abundance.

However, with all that in mind, I also believe that the kind of abundance Jesus was talking about is also for us to have the best of everything on this Earth. For example...

Jesus wants you to be healthy and happy.

He wants you to take good care of your body, mind, and spirit.

Let's go back to the words of Jesus; "The thief comes only to steal and kill and destroy; I came so that they would have life and have it abundantly."

I already told you what I believe Jesus was talking about, that concerns your soul and salvation.

Most Bible experts agree that the thief in that context is Satan. And the abundant life Jesus was talking about concerns your abundant life in heaven. I agree with all of that. However...

What if the "thief" Jesus was talking about two thousand years ago is now working in an entirely different way?

Could that be possible?

Let's look at this story from the perspective of diet and health.

To do that, we must return to the words I gave you at the start of this...

But I'm going to break-it-down and say those words in a different way.

Fact #1: We live in a world where politicians, in league with corporations, pursue their own interests with no genuine concern for the lives or livelihoods of the people they claim to serve.

Fact #2: Instead of trusting and empowering you to look after yourself and your family, politicians and corporations foster extreme dependency by peddling treatments for symptoms instead of solving the underlying problems.

Fact #3: These solutions include "Frankenstein Foods" (I love that phrase) and pills, while the types of nutritious life-preserving foods that sustained our ancestors for millennia are slandered and treated as the opposite.

There's much more to say, but can we agree on these 3 facts for now?

If not, please stop reading.

Think about each fact above.

Only continue when you can see the truth in those 3 statements.

Once you do that, you are ready to move on to the next fact...

Fact #4: This twisted regime does all these things and more in open furtherance of a plan to destroy the nations and usher in a new global form of

Up to $234 in Free Gifts at <u>JesusDietChallenge.com</u>

government, a form of tyranny that will be unlike any seen before.

I realize that last fact may sound like a conspiracy of some kind. It's not. These things are happening all over the globe, wherever you live.

The experts I follow call this "soy globalism," but what if this is all a result of the same thief that Jesus Christ was talking about in the Gospel of John?

Is this a stretch? Maybe. But I don't think so. I think we agree that the devil is alive and well in today's world. And it might be a simplistic view, but if we are what we eat or what we eat is doing to us, then anything that affects our health and makes us sick and fat and depressed and isolated is not the work of God and Jesus.

It is the sinister, evil work of the enemy.

The same negative force of evil that Jesus was talking about in John 10:10.

One thing is for sure; you and I are living in a world of good–vs–evil.

It's spiritual warfare.

And if you think about it in a general way, you'll see that this is true.

Jesus came that you should have life and have it more abundantly. That means Heaven and eternal life, for sure. But it also means an abundant life right here and now. It means having the best of everything while you are here on earth. And all that starts with your diet.

I believe that anything that promotes health and happiness is a thing of God.

And anything that promotes the opposite of all of that is of the devil.

But is it really that simple?

Good–vs–evil?

Yes, I believe it is.

I think that what the powers-that-be call health care is really just sick care.

I believe that the foods and lifestyle choices that are being promoted to us are making us sick. Some of us just aren't showing any symptoms yet.

I was talking about this yesterday with my good friend and mentor Russ von Hoelscher, and he said these words: "Dead people don't pay their bills!" Brilliant!

In other words, "big pharma" and "big food" don't want to kill you.

But they don't exactly want you to be healthy and happy, either.

What they want is for you is to be fat, sick, depressed, and isolated.

Only then can they control you in the most extreme way. If some people die, that's fine. After all, to them, you are only a number. What do you care when a small percentage die? It's only business, right? They make more money if you're alive, sure. However, they make zero money if you are healthy and happy and unified.

Can you see how the thief that Jesus was talking about could be behind all of this?

Jesus came so that you should have life and have it more abundantly.

The opposite of abundance is scarcity and lack and limitations.

It's never having enough.

It's being sick and tired and isolated.

And this is where our politicians, in league with corporations, pursue their own interests with no genuine concern for the lives or the livelihoods of you and me.

It's pure evil. The stuff of that thief and enemy of God, the devil himself.

I believe this is exactly the kind of evil Jesus was talking about...

It is the evil that steals your health.

It destroys your health, happiness, and well-being.

It makes you less effective as a follower of Jesus.

It keeps you from being all you can be.

It stops you from being a force for good.

It limits you in every meaningful way.

People who are strong and happy don't need a bunch of drugs. We only need medications in the most temporary ways. We don't need hospital visits and surgeries.

Jesus came to heal us of all of that.

I realize that telling you about the evil forces and the power that is inside the food and medical profession is a bit controversial.

But Jesus came to heal the sick. That means the abundance he was talking about was also about the here and now. It's not only about eternal salvation or eternal life. It's being happy and healthy and strong while we're still in this world.

You can be used by God in the fullest way when you are at your best.

To sum it up, only the devil would want you to be fat, sick, depressed, overly medicated, and isolated from other strong Christians.

It may have sounded like a conspiracy theory at first. But when you add it up, you'll see. People who are weak and sick are easily influenced. And easy to control. Sick, depressed, and isolated people are a danger to themselves and others. The overly processed foods that cause many people to become fat, sick, and depressed have become a tool for Satan to control people and do his evil bidding.

If you want to be a tool for God, you will do things that make you strong and healthy and full of life and energy. That starts with your diet and lifestyle.

The stronger you are, the less the devil can use you. God is a force of good. God is positivity. God's spirit in you is a spirit of strength and power. He wants you to be positive, loving and the kind of person who leads others to Jesus.

Any diet that gives you more strength, more health, more vitality, and more energy is the type of diet that Jesus would want for you.

Strong and healthy people can be depended on. They are a positive force. They build, create, love, and give. Jesus wants you to be healthy and happy. He wants you to be a force for good. He wants you to be the very best you can possibly be; to give, serve, love, inspire, encourage and give strength to other people.

That's what The Jesus Diet is; the type of good that He

would want for you.

Jesus wants you to be strong and healthy.

Strong people live with purpose and passion. They add value. They lift people up instead of tearing them down. They hold themselves to a higher standard.

When you are strong, God can use you in the greatest way.

Sick, fat, weak, depressed, addicted, unhappy, and isolated people have nothing positive to offer. All they do is take. Strong people are disciplined, motivated and extremely focused. They practice self-control. They become God's tools. And that is what this diet is all about...

Now let me tie all this together. First, The Jesus Diet is a form of Intermittent Fasting. And one of the things that people love about this type of daily fasting is the fact that you can eat whatever you want to eat and still lose weight. However, I believe...

Jesus would only want you to eat foods that heal, not foods that kill.

Jesus would also want you to be on a diet that encourages prayer and meditation.

Jesus would want a diet that made you healthy and happy... so you could bring more people into His kingdom.

And with all that said, let me back up and tell you...

How I discovered The Jesus Diet.

This diet began when I first began to practice Intermittent Fasting.

This form of daily fasting changed my life. It helped me

lose weight, feel better, and have more energy. I became convinced that it was helping me to avoid certain diseases that happen to people like me as they get older (I was in my early 60's when I first started this diet) and most importantly, this diet was helping me get closer to God.

I fell in love with this diet. I decided to practice it for the rest of my life.

I have always struggled with my weight, and this was the "instant" weight loss solution that I always wanted. Finally, I didn't have to count calories or watch what I ate. I didn't have to take a bunch of diet pills and powders... And I felt so good about it and wanted to share it with all my friends.

But I quickly discovered why this diet is hard for many people.

I'll tell you why in a minute.

You see, there's a huge problem that causes many people to quit this diet.

And in the early days, this was a mighty problem for me, too...

But then I solved this problem.

And I wrote the original manual about it, called...

The 5-Hour Miracle Diet.

This diet lets you eat whatever you want and still lose weight.

Plus, it's been proven to help you live longer and avoid certain diseases…

It's scientific. This diet is backed by extensive medical research. In fact, to write this, I had to boil down thousands of pages of scientific and medical studies...

It's even spiritual. The positive benefits you'll experience on this diet will spill over into every other area of your life. And that includes your relationship with God...

I'll tell you all the facts.

Be prepared to be shocked and amazed. You'll discover why I first called this the 5-Hour Miracle Diet and why I believe it is helping me to live longer, adding life to my remaining years, and bringing me closer to God. It can do these things for you. Plus, it can even make you money as you help other people discover the benefits of this life-changing diet... I can't wait to tell you more about that!

This diet is a form of daily fasting that most people call intermittent fasting. It's simple. I just skip breakfast and eat two meals, the first around 12:30 pm and the second around 6:30 pm. Then, I fast for the rest of the night.

It's that simple.

And it works: this simple activity tricks my brain into thinking that I am fasting for more extended periods, and that has (over time) changed my metabolism. Because of this, I can eat all the foods I love and still lose weight....

The Jesus Diet takes this to a whole new level, by striving to eat the best food.

With this unique form of daily fasting, I've not only lost weight, but I feel better and have more energy. It changed my life because I sleep better each night, and it helps me deal with the problems and the stress of building my growing business. Plus, it has helped me get closer to God. It can help you do all this, too.

The only challenge you'll face is the time each day when

you are hungry.

That's why I called this the 5-Hour Miracle Diet. I have much to tell you about this problem and the secret that solves it later... For now, you may wonder...

HOW IS ALL THIS EVEN POSSIBLE?

How can you get miraculous results on a diet this simple? Isn't skipping breakfast bad for you? Why would anyone fast for 16 to 18 hours every day? What are the long-term benefits? Is there any science behind this? Is it dangerous?

Slow down, friend. I've tried some crazy diets, but this isn't one of them. It's easy to add this to your lifestyle and it has many health benefits. I'll go over the main health benefits and show you how this can change your life.

This type of fasting is different from all other diets. It's technically not a diet. Instead, it's a pattern of eating. It's a way of scheduling your meals to get the most out of them. This doesn't change what you eat; it changes when you eat.

You can get lean without cutting your calories. You'll usually try to keep your calories the same when you start fasting. (Most people eat bigger meals during a shorter time frame.) Plus, it is a great way to keep your muscle mass while getting lean.

> This unique type of fasting is one of the best strategies for taking bad weight off while keeping good weight on because you don't have to change your life.
>
> It's the perfect diet for you because this type of fasting is simple enough that you'll do it, but meaningful enough that it will make a difference.

How The Jesus Diet Works

To understand how this type of fasting leads to fat loss, you first need to understand the difference between the <u>fed</u> states and <u>fasted</u> states.

Your body is in the <u>fed state</u> when it is digesting and absorbing food. Typically, the fed state starts when you begin eating and lasts for three to five hours as your body digests and absorbs the food you just ate. <u>When you are in the fed state, it's difficult for your body to burn fat because your insulin levels are high.</u>

After that timespan, your body goes into what's known as the post-absorptive state, which is just a fancy way of saying that your body isn't processing a meal.

The fasted state lasts until 8 to 12 hours after your last meal. These are the periods when your body becomes a fat-burning furnace!

Here's why: It is much easier for your body to burn fat in the fasted state because your insulin levels are low.

When you're in the fasted state, your body can burn fat that has been inaccessible during the fed state.

Because you don't enter the fasted state until 12 hours after your last meal, your body is rarely in this <u>fat-burning state</u>. This secret lets you lose fat without changing what you eat, how much you eat, or how often you exercise.

In other words, fasting puts your body in a fat-burning state that you rarely make it to during a regular eating schedule.

Fat loss is great, but it isn't the only benefit of this diet...

1. It simplifies your day.

I'm big on behavior change, simplicity, and reducing stress.

Daily fasting provides additional simplicity to my life that I enjoy. When I wake up, I don't worry about breakfast. I just grab a cup of black coffee and start my day.

I eat one less meal, which also means planning one less meal, cooking one less meal, and stressing about one less meal. It makes my life a bit simpler, and I like that.

2. It helps you live longer.

Scientists have long known that restricting calories is a way to lengthen your life. From a logical standpoint, this makes sense. When you're starving, your body finds ways to extend your life.

But who wants to starve themselves to live longer? I don't know about you, but I'm interested in enjoying a long life. I want to eat the foods I love! Restricting my calories by eating terrible 'diet food' is not an enjoyable way to live.

The good news is that fasting activates many of the same mechanisms for extending life as calorie restriction. In other words, you get the benefits of a longer life without the hassle of starving.

This diet has been shown to extend the lifespan and reduce age-related diseases in animals. A recent study found that multiple genes associated with longevity were enhanced by people who followed a time-restricted eating plan in which all meals were consumed between 8 a.m. and 2 p.m.

3. It may reduce the risk of cancer.

This one is up for debate because there hasn't been a lot of research and experimentation done on the relationship between cancer and fasting. Early reports, however, look positive.

This study of cancer patients suggests that the side effects of chemotherapy may be diminished by fasting before treatment.

This finding is also supported by another study that used alternate day fasting with cancer patients and concluded that fasting before chemotherapy would result in better cure rates and fewer deaths.

Cancer-fighting properties

One study on women found diet-induced biochemical changes in breast tissue that researchers interpreted as potentially protective against breast cancer (the women also lost weight). Research suggests that fasting-mimicking diets (like this one!) could make cancer cells more vulnerable to treatment.

This comprehensive analysis of many studies on fasting and disease has concluded that fasting appears to reduce the risk of cancer and cardiovascular disease.

4. It is much easier than dieting.

The reason most diets fail isn't that you switch to the wrong foods; it's because you don't follow the diet over the long term. It's not a nutrition problem; it's a behavior change problem.

This is where daily fasting shines because it's remarkably easy to implement once you get over the idea that you must eat all the time. For example, one study found that daily fasting was an effective strategy for weight loss in obese adults and concluded that "subjects quickly adapt" to a regular fasting routine.

I like the quote below from Dr. Michael Eades, on the difference between trying a diet and trying daily fasting.

"Diets are easy in the contemplation, difficult in the execution. Daily fasting is just the opposite – it's difficult in the contemplation but easy in the execution.

Most of us have gone on a diet. When we find a diet that

appeals to us, it seems as if it will be a breeze to do. But it becomes challenging when we do it. For example, I stay on a low–carb diet almost all the time. But if I think about going on a low–fat diet, it looks easy. I think about bagels, whole wheat bread, and jelly, mashed potatoes, corn, bananas by the dozen, etc. – all of which sound appealing. But were I to embark on such a low–fat diet, I would soon tire of it and wish I could have meat and eggs. So a diet is easy in contemplation but not so easy in the long–term execution.

Fasting every day is hard to contemplate. "You go without food for 16 to 18 hours a day?" people would ask when we explained what we were doing. "I could never do that." But once started, it's a snap. No worries about what and where to eat for one or two out of the three meals per day. It's a great liberation. You spend less on food. And you're not particularly hungry. …Although it's tough to overcome the idea of going without food, once you begin, nothing could be easier."

The ease of this diet is the best reason to do it. It lets you eat good food and still lose weight without forcing you to change too much.

5. Reduced inflammation

This diet lets you protect yourself from the damage of chronic inflammation. Several human studies demonstrate fasting's effectiveness at fighting oxidative stress and inflammation – two drivers of aging and chronic disease.

How this diet turns your body into a fat-burning machine.

The food you eat is broken down by enzymes in your gut and ends up as molecules in your bloodstream. Carbohydrates, particularly sugars and refined grains (think white flour and rice), are quickly broken down into sugar, which your cells use for energy. If your cells don't use it all, you store it in your fat cells as, well, fat.

But sugar can only enter your cells with insulin, a hormone made in the pancreas. Insulin brings sugar into your fat cells and keeps it there.

Between meals, as long as you don't snack, your insulin levels will go down, and your fat cells can then release their stored sugar to be used as energy.

You lose weight if you let your insulin levels go down. The entire idea of IF is to allow the insulin levels to go down far enough and for long enough that you burn off your fat. That's the secret that lets you eat whatever you want and still lose weight.

It's simple. It works. And the health benefits will change your life.

I try to follow an 18–hour fast followed by a 6–hour eating period.

It doesn't matter when you start your eating period. You can begin at 8 am and stop at 4 pm. Or you start at 2 pm and stop at 10 pm. Do whatever works for you. I tend to find that eating around 12:30 pm and 6:30 pm works well because those times allow me to eat lunch and dinner with friends and family. Breakfast is typically a meal I eat on my own, so skipping it isn't a big deal.

Because this kind of fasting is done every day, it becomes very easy to get into the habit of eating on this schedule. You're probably eating around the same time every day without thinking about it. Daily fasting is the same thing; you learn not to eat at certain times, which is remarkably easy.

While I have practiced fasting consistently for several years, I'm not fanatical about my diet. With The Jesus Diet, I strive to eat the very best food I possibly can. My entire focus is to build healthy habits that guide my behavior 90% of the time so that I can do whatever I feel like during the other 10%. If I come to your house to watch a movie and you want to fix me something to eat at 9 pm, guess what? I don't care that it's outside my eating period; I'm eating it. And when I do cheat and eat foods that I know Jesus would not want me to eat, I pray for forgiveness and strive to do better the next day.

"This is crazy. I'd die if I didn't eat for 16 to 18 hours a day!"

The mental barrier is your only real obstacle. This prevents people from trying any kind of diet that includes fasting. But once you get past that, and once you try it and see the amazing results, and once it becomes a habit and a permanent part of your life, it's easy to do. For now, know this...

Why this diet isn't as crazy as you may think it is...

>> *First*, fasting has been practiced by various religious groups for centuries. Medical practitioners have also noted the health benefits of fasting for thousands of years. In other words, fasting isn't some new fad or a crazy marketing ploy. It's been around for a long time, and it works.

>> *Second*, fasting may seem strange to you because nobody talks about it. To understand why that is, all you have to do is follow the money. Nobody makes money by telling you not to eat their products, not take their supplements, or not buy their goods. In other words, fasting is not a very marketable topic, so you're not exposed to advertising and marketing about it. The result is that it seems somewhat extreme or strange, even though it's not.

>> *Third*, you've probably already fasted many times. For example, have you ever slept in late on the weekends and then had a late brunch? Some people do this every weekend. In situations like these, you often eat dinner the night before and then don't eat until 11 am, noon, or even later. There's your 16–

hour fast, and you didn't even think about it.

Technically this isn't a "diet" because you will focus less on your overall caloric intake and more on restricting your eating to specific periods each day. For the most part, that's just common sense – and the health benefits can be huge if you're accustomed to eating all day (and night) long. *In short,*

It's not what you eat, but when you eat.

With this type of fasting, you only eat during a specific time. Fasting for a certain number of hours each day or eating just one meal a couple of days a week will help your body burn fat. And scientific evidence points to some amazing health benefits, as well.

Neuroscientist Mark Mattson has studied fasting for 25 years. He says that your body has evolved to go without food for many hours, or even several days or longer. Before humans learned to farm in prehistoric times, they were hunters and gatherers who evolved to survive – and thrive – for long periods without eating. They had to: It took a lot of time and energy to hunt game and gather nuts and berries.

Even 50 years ago, it was easier to maintain a healthy weight. Dietitian Christie Williams explains: "There were no computers, and TV shows turned off at 11 p.m.; people stopped eating because they went to bed. Portions were much smaller. More people worked and played outside and generally got more exercise.

Nowadays, TV, the internet, and other entertainment are available 24/7. We stay awake for longer hours to catch our favorite shows, play games, and chat online. We're sitting and snacking all day – and most of the night."

Extra calories and less activity mean a higher risk of obesity, type 2 diabetes, heart disease, and other illnesses. Scientific studies show that fasting every day may help reverse these trends.

It's so simple to do this diet. And it will change your life...

>>   There are several different ways to do this kind of fasting, but they are all based on choosing regular periods to eat and fast.

>>   After hours without food, your body uses its sugar stores and starts burning fat.

>>   Some experts call this metabolic switching.

If you are eating three meals a day, plus snacks, and you're not exercising, then every time you eat, you're running on those calories and not burning your fat stores.

Fasting every day works by prolonging the period when your body has burned through the calories consumed during your last meal and begins burning fat.

But The Jesus Diet does more than burn fat. Because when changes occur with this metabolic switch, it affects your body and brain. Many studies have proven that the various health benefits associated with fasting add up to...

A longer life, leaner body, and sharper mind.

According to my research, many things happen during this type of fasting that can protect your organs against chronic diseases like type 2 diabetes, heart disease, age-related disorders, even inflammatory bowel disease, and many cancers.

Here are a few more of the fasting benefits that research has revealed so far:

>>   Thinking and memory. Studies discovered that fasting boosts working memory in animals and verbal memory in adult humans.

>> Heart health. Daily fasting improved blood pressure, resting heart rates, and other heart-related measurements.

>> Physical performance. Young men who fasted for 16 hours showed fat loss while maintaining muscle mass. Others showed better endurance in running.

>> Diabetes and obesity. In animal studies, daily fasting prevented obesity. And in studies, obese adult humans lost weight through daily fasting.

And when you consider everything in this, you'll see...

People use this method to lose weight, improve their health, get closer to God, and simplify their life in every way.

Fasting has been a practice throughout human evolution. Ancient hunter-gatherers didn't have supermarkets, refrigerators, or food available year-round. Sometimes they couldn't find anything to eat.

As a result, we evolved to function without food for long periods.

Fasting is more natural than always eating 3–4 (or more) meals per day.

Fasting is also often done for spiritual reasons, which is the focus of this diet...

There are several ways you can do this diet, all of which involve splitting your day into eating and fasting periods.

During the fasting periods, you eat nothing at all.

The most popular way to do this is called the 16/8 method: It involves skipping breakfast and restricting your daily eating period to 8 hours, such as 1–9 p.m. Then you fast for 16 hours in between.

Many people find the 16/8 method to be the easiest to stick to. It's also the most popular. I try to push it to 18/6, which means, for example, I try to start eating at 1 p.m. and stop at 7 p.m. It all takes some getting used to. But once it becomes a habit, it does get easier. You'll feel better because you are eating healthier food. Plus, once you experience the thrill of turning your body into a fat-burning machine (and the spiritual benefits), you will be highly motivated to continue it!

The Science Behind This Diet.

Several things happen in your body on the cellular level when you fast:

>> Your body adjusts hormone levels to make stored body fat accessible.

>> Your cells initiate essential repair processes.

>> Your human growth hormone levels go up, and insulin levels go down. Your body's cells also initiate critical cellular repair processes.

But that's only the beginning...

>> Better concentration: Okay, the connection between fasting and your body health looks promising, but what about your brain health? Some animal studies have shown this kind of fasting to be protective to your brain by improving its function and structure, like in a recent study in Experimental Biology and Medicine, which suggests fasting may protect you against Alzheimer's disease by reducing the incidence of memory loss.

>> Lower cholesterol: One of the reasons fasting leads to weight loss is because you're eating during daytime hours when your body naturally wants to

consume calories. According to my research, when you eat according to your circadian rhythm – meaning you consume energy during your active hours of the day when the sun is up and eat less in the evening – you metabolize your food better and see improvements in blood sugar and cholesterol levels.

>> Better sleep: Scientists have been studying the effects of food intake on sleep for years. This research has shown that eating late at night can disrupt sleep or cause sleep disturbances. Many say that daily fasting is helping them sleep better than they have in years.

>> Reduced inflammation: The Yale School of Medicine studied the effects of fasting and diets on the body's macrophages, or inflammatory immune cells, and found that low-carb dieting, fasting, or high-intensity exercise may help to reduce that kind of inflammatory response.

>> Mindful eating habits: Ever reach for a candy bar or bag of chips without realizing what you're doing? Of course! That's called mindless eating, and we've all done it. But do it often enough, and it can cause you to fall out of step with your body's natural hunger cues. Many people eat emotionally, particularly at night when it's easy to sit in front of the TV and mindlessly consume extra calories. But this diet forces you to establish clear eating periods. This lets you stop your absent-minded snacking and can help you take in fewer calories.

>> Better immunity: Some proponents of fasting have claimed that restricting caloric intake for even a short period can "reset" your immune system, giving it a much-needed power boost. This theory was born from a University of Southern California study, which suggested that fasting for 72 hours could allow your body to flush out damaged

immune <u>cells</u> and <u>regenerate</u> new, <u>healthier</u> <u>cells</u> <u>primed</u> <u>to</u> <u>help</u> <u>the</u> <u>body</u> <u>fight</u> <u>toxins</u>. (The effects of fasting on chemotherapy patients were examined in this study.). It only makes sense that if these results can be achieved on an extended fast, you could potentially get these same health benefits through daily fasting over a prolonged period.

>> Delayed aging: Can building your daily schedule around fasting add years to your life? I believe it can! That is a lofty claim and hasn't been studied carefully enough in humans. Still, one study in Cell Metabolism found that alternate day fasting, specifically, did improve some of the more common markers of aging—like cardio health and fat-to-lean ratio—in a small sample of healthy, non-obese people. This is so important; *I must say it again...*

This amazing diet may help you live longer.

Making fasting a part of your daily life could extend your lifespan.

That's a bold statement. But there is plenty of science to back this up. For example, daily fasting has also been shown to increase the life of certain animals.

In some of these studies, the effects were quite dramatic.

In an older study, rats that fasted every other day lived 83% longer than rats that didn't fast. In another study, mice that fasted every other day saw their lifespans increase by around 13%. Fasting was also shown to improve their overall health. It helped delay the onset of conditions such as fatty liver disease and hepatocellular carcinoma, which are both common in aging mice. Although this is far from being determined in humans, these proven results from animal testing make this a popular diet for anyone who wants to add years to their life. Given the known benefits of metabolism and other health benefits that I will tell you about, it makes sense that this diet could help you live a longer and healthier life.

>> Clearer skin: What you eat affects your skin health. The American Academy of Dermatology confirms that certain foods, like milk, white bread, and sugary snacks or beverages, can increase acne by spiking your blood sugar. But can the time of day you eat affect your skin health, too? I am sure it can. Right now, the evidence is primarily anecdotal, based on what we know about the combined factors that can cause acne, like inflammation, high levels of insulin, and lack of restorative "beauty" sleep. Because fasting may help with some of these root causes of acne, it could—in theory—be a solution to common skin issues.

>> Help for diabetes: Type 2 diabetes has become a common diagnosis in recent decades. Its main feature is high blood sugar levels in the context of insulin resistance. Anything that reduces insulin resistance in your body should help lower blood sugar levels and protect you against type 2 diabetes.

>> Heart health: Heart disease is the world's biggest killer. Regular periods of fasting have been shown to decrease the risk of heart disease.

>> Cellular health: Fasting helps to repair the cells in your body.

Here's how: When you fast, the cells in your body initiate a cellular "waste removal" process called autophagy. This involves your cells breaking down and metabolizing broken and dysfunctional proteins that build up inside your cells over time. Increased autophagy may give you protection against several diseases, including cancer and neurodegenerative diseases such as Alzheimer's disease. Fasting triggers a metabolic pathway called autophagy, which removes waste material from your cells.

>> May help prevent cancer: Cancer is characterized by uncontrolled growth of cells. Fasting has been shown to have several beneficial effects on metabolism that may help you reduce your cancer risk. Promising evidence from animal studies indicates that daily fasting or diets that mimic long-term fasting may help prevent cancer. There's also some evidence showing that fasting reduced various side effects of chemotherapy in humans.

>> Brain health: What's good for the body is also good for the brain.

Daily fasting improves various important metabolic features for your overall brain health. Several animal studies have shown that daily fasting may increase the growth of new nerve cells, which should benefit your brain's function. Fasting also increases a brain hormone called brain-derived neurotrophic factor (BDNF). A BDNF deficiency has been implicated in depression and various other brain problems. Animal studies have also shown that fasting protects against brain damage due to strokes. Fasting may increase the growth of new neurons and protect your brain from damage.

>> May help prevent Alzheimer's disease: Alzheimer's is the world's most common neurodegenerative disease. There's no cure currently available for Alzheimer's, so preventing it from showing up in the first place is critical. Animal studies show that fasting may delay the onset of Alzheimer's or reduce its severity. In a series of case reports, a lifestyle intervention that included daily short-term fasts significantly improved Alzheimer's symptoms

in 9 out of 10 people. Animal studies suggest that fasting may protect against other neurodegenerative diseases, including Parkinson's and Huntington's. These studies indicate that fasting may protect against all neurodegenerative diseases.

But the most attractive benefit to this diet may be that it can help you lose all the weight you want and still eat the very best food. To help you understand the reason why let me give you...

The Secret to Weight Loss.

To lose weight, you must eat fewer calories than you burn.

It's that simple.

Refuse to let anyone else tell you anything different.

Your body obeys the laws of <u>thermodynamics</u>, which means that you must burn more calories than you consume regularly to lose weight.

Every day, your body needs a certain number of calories to carry out its daily functions: making your heart beat, your brain function, getting your body to move, and all sorts of other things. This is called your total daily energy expenditure.

>> When you consume more calories than you burn, your body stores those extra calories as fat (weight gain).

>> When you burn more calories than you consume, your body will pull from fat stores for energy (weight loss).

To lose weight, you must find a way to tip the energy balance in your favor and turn your body into a fat-burning machine.

You must eat less and move more to get your body to turn your fat into energy.

Unfortunately, that's where the problems start.

Like most people, you are good at underestimating how much you eat and overestimating how many calories you burn.

When you eat more calories than you think you are and burn fewer calories from exercise than you assume, you think you "can't lose weight" because of your metabolism or genetics. That's not true. Because...

The real problem: you eat more than you should.

The Jesus Diet is the solution.

Here's why: By cutting out an entire meal each day, you are consuming fewer calories – even if your two meals per day are slightly bigger than before. Overall, you're still consuming fewer calories per day. In this example, you're eating larger lunches and dinners than usual, but by skipping breakfast, you'll consume 500 fewer calories.

And after a while, that adds up to weight loss!

Then, over time, it can change your entire metabolism, which can cause your body to calories like a hot furnace!

It's that simple. This works. Science proves it. However, let me clarify and help you understand how this can change your life. *For starters...*

Daily fasting will change your life because your body operates differently when "feasting" than "fasting."

Remember, when you eat a meal, your body spends a few hours processing that food, burning what it can from what you just consumed.

Because it has all of this readily available, easy-to-burn energy (thanks to the food you ate), your body will choose to use that as energy rather than the fat you have stored.

During the "fasted state" (the hours in which your body is not consuming or digesting any food), your body doesn't have a recently consumed meal to use as energy.

Thus, it is more likely to pull from the fat stored in your body as it's the only energy source readily available.

When your body is in a fasted state, it is forced to adapt and pull from a source of energy that it does have available: the fat stored in your cells.

That's how this diet works...

Now let me tell you why this works:

Your body reacts to energy consumption (eating food) with insulin production.

The more sensitive your body is to insulin, the more likely you'll be to use the food you consume efficiently. And that's where the fat-burning miracle of daily fasting comes in because your body is most sensitive to insulin following a period of fasting.

These insulin production and sensitivity changes can help lead to weight loss and muscle creation.

Next: Your glycogen (a starch stored in your muscles and liver that your body can burn as fuel when necessary) is depleted during sleep (aka during fasting), and will be depleted even further during your waking periods when you are fasting, which can lead to increased insulin sensitivity.

This means that the food you eat after you've gone through your daily fasting period will be used more efficiently. It will be converted to glycogen and stored up in your muscles or burned as energy immediately to help with recovery, with minimal amounts stored as fat.

Compare this to a regular day (with no fasting): With insulin sensitivity at normal levels, the carbs and foods you consume will see full glycogen stores and enough glucose in your bloodstream, and thus be more likely to get stored as fat.

But all that is different when you fast.

Why? It's because growth hormone is increased when your body is in a fasted state (both during sleep and after your period of fasting). Combine this increased growth hormone secretion and the decrease in insulin production (and thus increase in insulin sensitivity), and you're essentially turning your body into a fat-burning machine.

To put it another way:

Daily fasting will train your body to use the food it consumes more efficiently. Your body will learn to burn fat as fuel when you deprive it of new calories to constantly pull from (as your body does when you eat all day long).

Daily fasting can be difficult. That's why we created our membership. More about that later.

Add it all up. You'll see. This diet can change your life. It can help you...

- Lose all the weight you want.

- Look and feel better.

- Have more energy and vitality.

- Sleep better.

- And even live longer!

That's a tall order. I know. But if you've read closely, you know it's true.

You've also seen how this can turn your body into a fat-burning furnace.

The Jesus Diet will turn up the volume on your metabolism and help you to lose weight and so much more. It could even save your life. I'm serious. My friend, Jay, may have saved my life (or added years to my life) when he told me about the benefits of daily fasting. Before this, I had tried all kinds of crazy diets, but fasting every day is different because it's based on this premise...

It's not what you eat; it's when you eat.

With this diet, you go through a significant daily period where you're not eating. You already do this when you're sleeping. So, if you sleep 8 hours a day, you're not consuming any calories during those hours. And if you're like most people, you're not hungry when you wake up. So going 10 to 12 hours without any calories is easy. Stretching it to 18 hours without food can be much more challenging. But in a moment, I'll begin to reveal the ultimate secret to dealing with the hunger. Remember, your goal is to stretch your fasting period for as long as possible.

I called this the 5-Hour Diet because of my unique perspective on intermittent fasting. I can't wait to help you to understand this. Not only can this change your life, but I'm convinced it can save your life and add years to your life, add life to your years!

This diet will give you more energy and vitality. It changes your metabolism and turns your body into a fat-burning machine! I know that sounds like hype, but it's true. I called it the 5-Hour Diet because I realized (after years of experimenting with different ways of doing it) that the key to making this diet an essential part of your life is to learn how to deal with the short periods of hunger you'll go through every day.

This is the only challenge that you must learn how to overcome. That's the purpose of the Miracle Method.

If you can learn how to live with these small doses of daily pain, you can lose weight fast, live longer, and eat whatever you want. I'll help you make it easy. And this is proven to work. It's as simple as learning how to get through the 3 to 5 hours a day when you're experiencing a little hunger.

The idea behind the title I chose for this diet came from my friend, Jay.

Jay is the man who got me excited about daily fasting. Like me, he's been trying to maintain and lose weight for years. He's also tried all the various diets. Most have left him frustrated. But this diet is different because it's focused on when you eat and not what you eat. I was having a conversation with Jay about this diet, and I said:

"The trick to this diet is your ability to deal with a little pain or hunger every day. If you can do that, you can master this diet."

The title for this diet came from that conversation. Jay and I have tried many different diets; like most people trying to lose weight or maintain weight, you try everything. And I realized that the only real problem with this diet is, or the only obstacle, if you will, the only challenge, that's another good way of saying it, you must be willing to just put up with a bit of hunger every day.

Most people have never really been hungry. You'll hear them saying things like "I'm starving to death!" and other sayings. But you will experience hunger on this diet (for short periods). I will give you the ultimate way to deal with this pain.

Understand this: if you can get through those 3 to 5 hours a day (and you can!), then you can master this diet and change your life. It's that simple. And with enough practice, it's that easy. Get good at dealing with this hunger (which I will help you do), and you will turn your body into a fat-burning machine.

And that brings us to the big question...

Can you eat whatever you want and still lose weight?

With this diet, you are limiting the calories that you put in your body every day. Study after study shows that one of the big secrets to longevity is restricting the calories you consume each day. All diets try to achieve this. You are watching what you eat and trying to limit your calories.

My dad called salad rabbit food. He struggled with his weight all his life and died before he had to. He was 74 years old when he died. I am convinced that he could have easily added a decade or two to his life if he had just been on a diet instead of eating all the time and fasting for a significant period each day.

Some people take daily fasting to an extreme. They call it the Warrior Diet. They go 20 hours without eating each day. And they refer to the 4 hours a day they eat as their 'feeding window.' I hate that idea! It sounds like I'm a rat in a cage. The Jesus Diet focuses on the period when you are hungry each day. This is when your body is in the fasted mode and burning fat. These are the times...

You are Turning Your Body into a Fat-Burning Furnace!

It's simple and will change your life. Don't eat during these fat-burning periods. After that, you can eat whatever you want...

EAT WHAT YOU WANT.

You can eat pizza, pasta, cake, and cookies and still lose weight. That sounds hard to believe. But if you've been reading closely, you know that you can eat all kinds of 'junk food' and still lose weight because you consume fewer calories.

Naturally, you want to eat healthy food, too. You will be more aware of food, but here is the point; food loses its power over you. When you constantly shove food in your face, you tend to feel hungry all the time (but it's not the same kind of hunger you'll feel when you fast). However, you are also eating because you are bored or the fact that you've never disciplined yourself to eat any other way.

When you constantly eat, food has more power and control over you than it should have. But when you are on The Jesus Diet, food loses its power over you.

When you fast every day, you can't just eat junk food because your body now becomes more sensitive to junk food. But you don't have to eat carrots, salad, celery, and all those 'diet foods' either. You can eat anything you want and still lose weight!

This diet lets you focus on the time
each day when you are feeling hungry.

That's the magic time that turns your
body into a fat-burning furnace.

I equate it with the way an athlete goes to the gym. When you talk to athletes, you'll realize that they all interpret pain differently. Look at a long-distance runner, where they put their body through all kinds of the worst pain that you can even imagine. Some are in so much pain that they crawl over the s line. Most don't make it over the finish line on those long ultra-marathon runs of 50 to 100 miles through all kinds of rugged terrain. They have ambulances; doctors are right there to save their lives. <u>These</u> <u>people</u> <u>have</u> <u>a</u> <u>different</u> <u>way</u> <u>of</u> <u>defining</u> <u>what</u> <u>pain</u> <u>means</u>.

The phrase '5-Hour Miracle Diet' came from a conversation with the man who introduced me to daily fasting. We were both struggling with this diet and encouraging each other to stay on it. <u>This</u> <u>is</u> <u>one</u> <u>of</u> <u>the</u> <u>secrets</u> <u>to</u> <u>making</u> <u>daily</u> <u>fasting</u> <u>a</u> <u>permanent</u> <u>part</u> <u>of</u> <u>your</u> <u>life</u>. When this diet starts working for you, share it with as many others as possible. See if you can't get them to try it. Our simple referral system for Members rewards you for sharing this diet with others. I have much more to say about this later...

For now, know this:

>> You have mastered this diet if you can learn to live with a bit of hunger for 3 to 5 hours every day.

>> This gives you an easy way to limit the calories you consume on a daily basis.

>> It's so simple. You <u>start</u> eating as late in the day as possible and <u>stop</u> eating as soon as possible.

>> Then, you are willing to feel that hunger for just a few hours a day, but you change the definition of that hunger. What does that pain mean? You change the meaning, and you change your life!

Therefore, when you do feel the pain of hunger, you'll

remind yourself that this is where the 'fat-burning magic' is happening. Eventually, your metabolism will change, and you will start to lose weight. You find meaning in the few hours of hunger, change the meaning of that pain, and the benefits will amaze you!

Short-Term Pain, Long-Term Gain

Every person who regularly exercises learns to deal with pain. These people endure a little discomfort every day because they see it as the price they pay to achieve their desired results. This diet lets you tap into that same kind of discipline and focus. As you'll see, this can also help you get closer to Jesus. More on that in a minute...

It's simple. It's proven. And it's guaranteed to let you lose weight and keep it off. Remember, all I do is wait as long as possible to start eating and then stop as early as possible. I give myself a little bit of leniency because none of us are robots. I try to go through 18 hours of not eating and 6 hours of eating. Follow this simple plan, and the 3 to 5 hours of hunger you experience each day is a small price to pay for all the fantastic life-changing benefits you can achieve. I will teach you a powerful method to deal with the pain of hunger. This is short-term pain to get the long-term gain that can change your life.

This beats all other weight-loss options.

Daily fasting focuses on when you eat, not what you eat. No more counting calories. No more cutting out the foods you love. No more guilt! All you must do is get through the 3 to 5 hours a day when you feel the actual pain of hunger.

We focus on the hunger you feel when you're on this diet. This is the part that most people try to avoid. They don't like to feel hungry. But as you'll see, the small amount of pain from daily hunger can be a positive thing. It can make you feel alive!

> The pain I go through on this diet has never been a problem. Why? Because I've discovered a simple 3-step technique to overcome all of life's challenges. I call it the Miracle Method because, like this diet, it can create a miracle in your life.

The uncomfortable feelings of hunger only lasts for a few hours a day. It's something I will help you overcome. That's where my little-known method comes in. I discovered this method many years ago while going through extremely difficult personal problems. It's a method that helps you cope with all kinds of pain, including the small block of time you will feel intense hunger pains on this diet.

Most people don't stay on this diet because of these intense feeling of hunger. They try this diet (because it's so simple), but they _feel_ they can't endure the pain. Some of my students feel as if they will die! They have never felt this kind of hunger, and after a few days (or even one day), they shout, *"I CAN'T DO IT!"* and they quit. This stops them from losing weight and keeping it off. It also prevents them from getting all the other long-term health benefits of daily fasting...

But the pain of hunger will never be a problem for you.

The main reason you haven't heard about daily fasting is the fact that nobody makes money by telling you not to eat their products, not take their supplements, or not buy their products or services. In other words, fasting is not a very marketable topic, so you're not exposed to advertising and marketing about it.

The result is that it seems somewhat extreme or strange, even though it's not.

Fasting has been around for centuries. Medical practitioners have also noted the health benefits of fasting for thousands of years. In other words, daily fasting isn't some new fad or a crazy marketing ploy. It's been here for a long time, and it works.

But as you also know, most people try this diet for a few days or a week and say: "I have never felt this hungry!" or "I feel like I will starve to death!" or "I have never felt hunger this intense!" or "There's no way I can torture myself like this!" Or the best statement I have read so far...

"I'd rather die than be on this diet!"

This is the language of emotion. They're the kind of words that my students will write down when they use the first step of the Miracle Method. I am excited to show you how this works! Some people feel they're going to die. BUT FEELINGS LIE. That's what the Miracle Method helps you realize. And even though you feel that you may not be able to withstand the short periods of intense hunger...

YOU ARE WRONG!

People have been fasting for centuries. Your body is built to go without food for long periods. The physical pain of hunger comes and goes. You learn to live with the pain of hunger and even learn how to enjoy it. As you'll see, the Miracle Method will teach you how to turn that pain into power!

The 3-step Miracle Method lets you transform your hunger pain into an entirely different experience. This is a spiritual method that lets you make Jesus your partner and let Him remove whatever pain you're suffering from. It can also help you with the short periods of intense feelings of pain you'll experience on this diet. Follow this method, and you'll develop the ability to deal with the few hours of daily hunger, turn your body into a fat-burning furnace and get closer to Jesus. This is a diet that Jesus would want you to be on and the Miracle Method is a 3-step method that will bring you closer to Him.

A Personal Invitation

I hope you have enjoyed this Summary Edition of The Jesus Diet. What you have just read was taken from the first Chapter of my breakthrough book, The Jesus Diet. If you enjoyed this summary, I know you'll want to read my full book to get the rest of the story.

The Jesus Diet book has 12 Chapters:

Ch.1 – What Would Jesus Want You to Eat. (What you just read on the previous 44 pages.)

Ch.2 – How the Miracle Method Helps You Stay On This Diet.

Ch.3 – 28 Shocking Facts About What's Killing You and the People You Love.

Ch.4 – Why a Gluten-Free Diet Could Save Your Life.

Ch.5 – Why People Are Dying from Avoidable Diseases Caused by Obesity, Such as Diabetes, Heart Disease, and Cancer... and How You Can Avoid Being One of Them.

Ch.6 – Why the Government's "Food Pyramid" Should Be Called the "Food Tombstone."

Ch.7 – The Little-Known Health Benefits of Better Sleep.

Ch.8 – The True Cause of the #1 Killer... and How You Can Avoid It.

Ch.9 – Death Starts in Your Gut.

Ch.10 – The Easy and Fun 30-Minute Cure for Your Biggest Health Problem.

Ch.11 – Here are 76 Ways That Sugar Can Ruin Your Health.

Ch.12 – Is Jesus God?

What you have just read in this short book is only from the

first Chapter of our big 293-page book. You'll definitely want to read the big book and learn more about how the Miracle Method and other key components of the Jesus Diet help you achieve total physical, mental, and spiritual health and wellness. Chapter 2 of the big book, in particular, reveals the Miracle Method; a 3-step process that is the secret to staying on the Jesus Diet and achieving the better life you're aiming for.

Here's how to get your copy of the full Jesus Diet book and a free 3-month subscription to our Jesus Diet Challenge Newsletter.

1. **Order a copy of our 293-page The Jesus Diet book.** On the next page, you'll find an Order Form. Fill out the Form and send it to me to receive a copy of The Jesus Diet. It's also available through bookstores everywhere, but you won't get the free gifts worth $234. Plus, I'll add you to my list of subscribers to my Jesus Diet Challenge Newsletter for 3 months.

2. **Let me send you <u>3 free months</u> of my Jesus Diet Challenge Newsletter – even if you don't get the big book.** Even if you don't want to purchase a copy of our big book, The Jesus Diet, you can still claim a 3-month complimentary subscription to our Jesus Diet Challenge Newsletter. It's packed with helpful information about the Jesus Diet, our Miracle Method, and everything else we've discussed in this small book. You'll love it!

Don't miss out on the opportunity to transform your physical and spiritual health and wellbeing. *Take action now to continue your journey with the Jesus Diet!*

Jesus Diet 293-Page Book and Free Newsletter Order Form

YES, T.J.! I read your book and I'm ready to dive in deeper. Please send me a copy of your big Jesus Diet book and a 3-month subscription to your Jesus Diet Challenge Newsletter. You have proven to me that this diet is something unique and special. I must know more! The book is just $25 (free s/h) and includes your newsletter for 3 months. Or, if I'm not ready to buy the book today, I can start with a free 3-month subscription to your Jesus Diet Challenge Newsletter. Either way, you'll also include the valuable free gifts worth $234 with my first package. *So on that basis, sign me up!*

STEP #1: Choose your option.

❐ **Send me the FREE Jesus Diet Challenge Newsletter (a $37.25 value)!** You'll learn more about the Jesus Diet and Miracle Method over the next 3 months. There's no obligation to purchase the book or become a Member. **SEND NO MONEY! Enjoy this 3-month subscription as our gift to you.**

❐ **Send your Newsletter and 293-Page Book!** Enclosed is $<u>25</u>.

STEP #2: Provide your payment information.

Card Number _____ Expiration _____

Signature _____ Security Code _____

STEP #3: Give us your complete contact information.

Name _____ Address _____

City/State/Zip Code _____

Daytime Phone Number _____

Email Address _____

INSTRUCTIONS: Fill out this Form and MAIL or FAX it directly to us.

MAIL to: <u>Jesus Diet/DRN</u> • P.O. Box 198 • Goessel, KS 67053

Or FAX to: (316) 333-1941

Submitting this Form constitutes an acceptance of the terms on the back.

For Internal Use Only:

_____
Referral ID Number

Did You Enjoy This Book?
If So, Here's What to Do Next...

STEP ONE:

Decide to purchase a copy of our big 293-page book for just $25 (free s/h), or just take advantage of our free subscription to the Jesus Diet Challenge Newsletter for 3 months.

STEP TWO:

Fill out the Form on the other side of this page. Be sure to check whether you just want the free newsletter subscription or whether you want a copy of our big book.

STEP THREE:

Send the Form back to me right away. While you wait, be sure to check out www.JesusDietChallenge.com for additional information about this amazing diet. Plus, you'll also discover how to get up to $234 in valuable bonus gifts.

Submitting this Form constitutes an acceptance of these terms: I understand that these resources are made available for education only and it's up to me and my personal physician to decide how to act based on the information provided. By placing this order and becoming a subscriber, I give you express permission to contact me about my subscription, my account, or other interesting offers by mail, fax, phone (live or auto-dialer), SMS (text message), e-mail, or any other means necessary to communicate with me. I can opt-out any time. If I have any questions, I can connect with you by referencing this book and contacting your support desk at tickets@heytj.com or 620-869-7076.